Space Explorer

THE STARS

Patricia Whitehouse

Heinemann
LIBRARY

young
Explorer

www.heinemann.co.uk/library
Visit our website to find out more information about *Heinemann Library* books.

To order:

 Phone 44 (0)1865 888066

 Send a fax to 44 (0)1865 314091

 Visit the Heinemann Bookshop at **www.heinemann.co.uk/library** to browse our catalogue and order online.

First published in Great Britain by Heinemann Library, Halley Court, Jordan Hill, Oxford OX2 8EJ, part of Harcourt Education. Heinemann is a registered trademark of Harcourt Education Ltd.

Editorial: Jilly Attwood and Kate Bellamy
Design: Ron Kamen and Paul Davies
Picture Research: Ruth Blair and Sally Claxton
Production: Séverine Ribierre

Originated by Dot Gradations Ltd
Printed and bound in China by South China Printing Company

The paper used to print this book comes from sustainable resources.

ISBN 0 431 11343 2
08 07 06 05 04
10 9 8 7 6 5 4 3 2 1

British Library Cataloguing in Publication Data
Whitehouse, Patricia
The Stars – (Space Explorer)
523.8

A full catalogue record for this book is available from the British Library.

Acknowledgements
The Publishers are grateful to the following for permission to reproduce photographs: Corbis pp. **25** (Danny Lehman), **22** (Roger Ressmeyer), **4-5**, **6**, **14** (royalty free); David Malin p. **7** (UK Schmidt Telescope); Francis Diego p. **28**; Science Photo Library p. **24**; Science Photo Library pp. **21** (Chandra X-Ray Observatory/NASA), **20** (J-C Cuillandre), **16** (European Southern Observatory), **18** (Mark Garlick), **8**, **26** (Jerry Schad), **17**, **27** (Eckhard Slawik), **13**, **15** (Space Telescope Science Institute/NASA), **29** (Frank Zullo); NASA p. **23**; NASA p. **11** (C.Sarazin et al.); NOAO p. **10** (Chuck Claver, Nigel Sharp), **9** (David Talent), **12** (Nathan Smith)

Cover photo reproduced with permission of NASA/H.Richer

Our thanks to Stuart Clark for his assistance in the preparation of this book.

Every effort has been made to contact copyright holders of any material reproduced in this book. Any omissions will be rectified in subsequent printings if notice is given to the Publishers.

Contents

Words written in bold, **like this,** are explained in the Glossary.

 Find out more about space at www.heinemannexplore.co.uk.

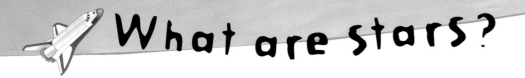

What are stars?

The night sky is full of stars. Each star looks like a tiny point of light. But stars are not really small.

They are huge balls of hot **gases**. They look small because they are so far away from the Earth.

The Sun is a star. It is the closest star to Earth but it is 150 million kilometres away.

The next closest star
to the Earth is called
Proxima Centauri.
It is more than
41 billion kilometres
further away
from Earth
than the Sun.

If you could drive a car
to the Sun, it would take
173 years to get there.
But it would take over
48 million years to drive
to the next closest star!

A **galaxy** is a huge group of stars. The Sun and many other stars we see are part of a huge group of stars called the Milky Way Galaxy.

There are over 200 billion stars in the Milky Way.

On a clear dark night, part of the Milky Way can be seen in the sky. The stars are so close together that they look like a white splash of milk across the sky.

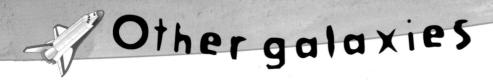

There are billions of **galaxies**. Most galaxies are very far away from Earth and can only be seen with a telescope.

Each of these bright spots is a galaxy containing billions of stars.

galaxy

This galaxy is round and flat, unlike the Milky Way.

Galaxies have many different shapes. The Milky Way is a spiral galaxy because it has a flat, spiral shape. Some galaxies are round. Other galaxies have no proper shape at all.

Stars start in huge clouds of **gas** in space. The gas squeezes together and gets very hot. The squeezed gas begins to glow and a star is born.

It takes millions of years for a new star to be made.

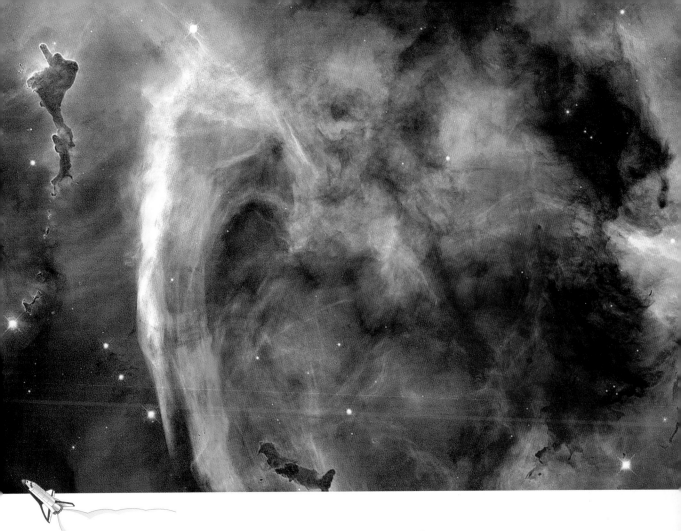

The bright spots are the new stars made in this nebula, called the **Eagle Nebula**.

A cloud of gas in space is called a **nebula**. A special telescope is needed to see the nebula and the new stars inside.

Star energy

In the middle of stars, **gas** is squeezed together so much that tiny parts of different gases join up. This makes powerful **nuclear energy**. Nuclear energy makes the stars hot and bright.

This group of stars is about 40 million years old.

Stars give out a lot of nuclear energy. In one second, a star like the Sun gives out as much energy as people would use in a million years.

People use nuclear energy from power plants to make heat and electricity on Earth.

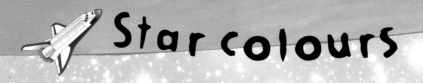

Star colours

Not all stars are yellow, like the Sun. Stars can be blue, white, or red too. A star's colour depends on its **temperature**.

The bright stars are young, red stars.

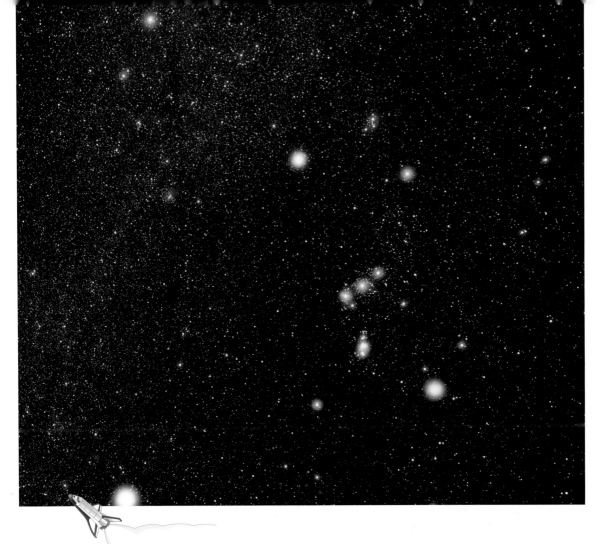

The outer parts of yellow stars can
get as hot as 6000°C.

Blue stars are the hottest, the next
hottest are white stars and then yellow
stars. The Sun is a yellow star. Stars
with the lowest temperature are red.

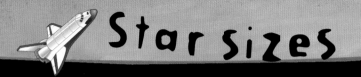

Sirius B

Earth

Over one million Earths could fit inside the Sun, but the Sun is not the biggest star. **Red giants** and supergiants are the largest stars. **White dwarfs** are small, hot stars.

Proxima Centauri

Sun

**Sirius B is a white dwarf and Proxima Centauri is
a red dwarf. They are both smaller than the Sun.**

After billions of years, stars use up their energy and change. Some smaller stars lose some of their **gases**, and then become **white dwarfs**.

The gases from a dying small star join together to make **nebulae**. This is where new stars may form.

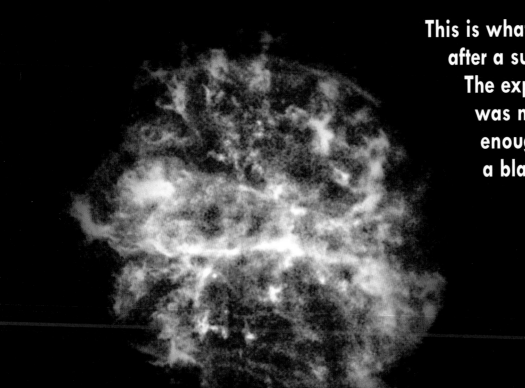

This is what was left after a supernovae. The explosion was not big enough to make a black hole.

Big stars explode. These huge explosions are called **supernovae**. A black hole might be all that is left after an explosion. In black holes **gravity** is so strong that not even light can escape.

Stars are round, like the Sun. But they do not seem round if you look at them from Earth. They look like twinkling points of light.

Stars seen from space do not twinkle because their light does not pass through the moving air around the Earth.

Stars twinkle because when we look at them we see their light through the moving air that is around the Earth. The moving air makes the starlight wiggle so it looks like the stars are twinkling.

23

Changing night sky

Long ago, people noticed that the stars in the sky changed place during the year. They also noticed that the stars came back to the same place at the same time every year.

People learned to use stars to work out the time. In South America, the stars showed the Maya people when it was time to plant crops.

This a ruin of an observatory the Maya people used in Mexico.

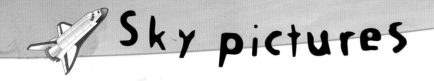

Sky pictures

People began to see shapes in groups of stars. They named the shapes and told stories to try to explain how the shapes were made.

**This group of stars is called the Plough.
Lines have been added to show its shape.**

This group of stars makes a 'w' shape. It is called Cassiopeia.

A group of stars that form a shape is called a **constellation**. Many constellations were named by the Ancient Greeks. Other cultures also had stories about constellations.

Orion is a **constellation** that looks like a man hunting. Some stars form a belt along the hunter's waist. A hunting knife hangs from the belt.

Lines have been added to show Orion's shape. Can you see his belt?

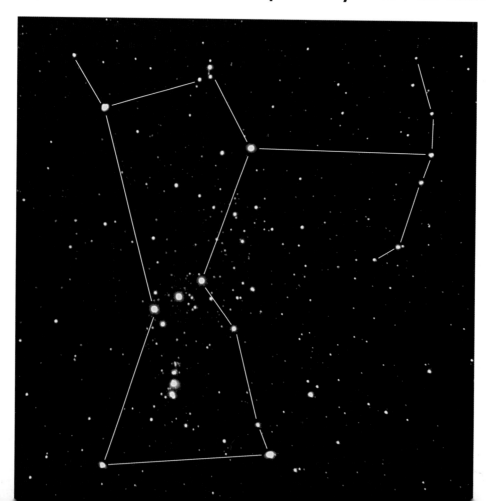

There is an ancient story from Greece about Orion the hunter. He was in love with a goddess named Diana but Orion died before they could marry. Diana put him in the sky as a group of stars to remember him.

This group of stars is named Scorpion, after the scorpion that was supposed to have killed Orion.

Amazing star facts

- Stars can last for billions of years.

- Scientists think there might be hundreds of billions of **galaxies** in the universe and each galaxy may have billions of stars.

- A **red giant** is 30 times bigger than the Sun.

- A brown dwarf is the smallest type of star.

Find out more about space at www.heinemannexplore.co.uk.

Glossary

constellation a group of stars that make a shape

galaxy a group of gases, dust and billions of stars

gas air-like material that is not solid or liquid

gravity a force that pulls objects together

nebula a cloud of gas in space where stars are made

nuclear energy when different parts of a gas join together to make powerful energy

red dwarf small star with a cool temperature

red giant very large star with a cool temperature

supernova when a very large star explodes

white dwarf small star with a hot temperature

More books and websites

The Sun (Space Explorer), Patricia Whitehouse (Heinemann Library, 2004)

www.esa.int
ww.nasa.gov/audience/forkids

Index

Titles in the *Space Explorer* series include:

Hardback   0 431 11347 5

Hardback   0 431 11348 3

Hardback   0 431 11345 9

Hardback   0 431 11342 4

Hardback   0 431 11341 6

Hardback   0 431 11344 0

Hardback   0 431 11343 2

Hardback   0 431 11340 8

Hardback   0 431 11346 7

Find out about the other titles in this series on our website www.heinemann.co.uk/library